Published by Creative Educational Society, Inc., 123 South Broad Street, Mankato, Minnesota 56001. Copyright © 1977 by Creative Educational Society, Inc. International copyrights reserved in all countries. No part of this book may be reproduced in any form without written permission from the publisher. Printed in the United States.
Library of Congress Cataloging in Publication Data
Paige, David.
Marlon Brando.
SUMMARY: A biography of a man who has earned the reputation for being not only a fine actor but a notorious rebel as well.
1. Brando, Marlon—Juvenile literature. 2. Moving-picture actors and actresses—United States—Biography—Juvenile literature. [1. Brando, Marlon. 2. Motion picture actors and actresses] I. Title.
PN2287.B683P3   791.43'028'0924 [B]   [92]   76-40690   ISBN 0-87191-552-9

Photo Credits: Grateful acknowledgement extended to:
Columbia Pictures, Metro Goldwyn Meyer, Paramount, 20th Century Fox, United Artists, Universal Studios, Warner Brothers, and Kenneth G. Lawrence and the movie Memorabilia Shop of Hollywood.

MARLON BRANDO

WRITTEN BY
DAVID PAIGE

DESIGNED BY
GENE KOHLER

CREATIVE EDUCATION
CHILDRENS PRESS

At 25 years old, Marlon Brando was ready to take on Hollywood and the movies. He was fresh from his sensational success in the Broadway play *A Streetcar Named Desire*.

The year was 1949, and Brando accepted an offer to make his first movie. On an uncomfortably hot summer day, he arrived in the movie capital of the world aboard the Santa Fe Super Chief.

Hollywood and the movie industry, on the other hand, were not prepared for Marlon Brando. On his first visit to the top executives at United Artists Studios, he was dressed in a T-shirt, levis, and tennis shoes.

But then Hollywood would never become accustomed to Marlon Brando. Twenty-four years later, when he won the Academy Award for best actor in *The Godfather,* it would be just as unprepared for him. When the "Oscars" were presented, he wasn't even there. In his place, he sent a young American Indian girl. Before the Academy Award audience and before the television cameras that were projecting the ceremonies to millions of people throughout the United States, she announced that he had refused to accept the award. She then read a short political statement from him about the way American Indians were being mistreated.

Hollywood had never seen anyone quite like Marlon Brando before. He was a rebel. He just did not behave the way everyone expected him to.

Brando did not drive around the city in a fancy, expensive car like the other stars. Instead he raced around the streets of Los Angeles on a motorcycle. He wasn't overwhelmed with awe at the already-established stars or the great producers and directors or the powerful executives of the studios. Instead he said that they were not making good movies in Hollywood. The good ones were all being made in Europe.

When the people in Hollywood expected him to be respectful, he played practical jokes. When they thought he should be seeking publicity like the other stars, he made every possible effort to avoid the writers and photographers who might put him in the newspapers and magazines.

U. S. 1959168

In those days, many thought that a star could be made or broken by the two most powerful columnists in Hollywood — Hedda Hopper and Louella Parsons. Actors and actresses treated the women with great respect in hope of earning a nice mention in their columns. Marlon Brando referred to Hedda Hopper as "the one with the hats" and Louella Parsons as "the fat one." He not only avoided them; but when he could not, he was downright rude to them.

Everyone had an opinion about Marlon Brando. Elia Kazan said he was "the gentlest man I've ever known." Ron Galella, a photographer, would not agree. He took a picture of Marlon on a street in New York. For it, Marlon punched him in the mouth. Galella went to the hospital with a broken jaw.

People in Hollywood tried to understand Marlon Brando, but they could not. Some thought he was putting them on, some thought he had not yet grown up, others thought he was insane. Most just did not know what to think, but there was one thing about him they learned quickly. He was an extraordinary actor.

Marlon Brando came to Hollywood from New York. However, he was actually born in Omaha, Nebraska, on April 3, 1924. He was the

third and last child of Marlon, Sr., and Dorothy Brando. He had two older sisters, Jocelyn and Frances.

The Brandos were not truly wealthy, but they were not poor either. They had a full-time, live-in maid. Marlon's father was a salesman. His mother, Dorothy, ran the household. She also had a very strong outside interest — she loved the theater, and she took a very active part in the community theater in Omaha. Tirelessly she tried to get new people to act in the theater. In the late 1920's, one of the persons she talked into trying his hand at acting was a young college drop-out from the Universty of Minnesota. His name was Henry Fonda.

Marlon Brando was a blond-haired, good-looking, and sometimes noticeably pudgy little boy. His parents called him "Bud." The nickname stuck with him for many years.

When he was ready to enter first grade, he did so in Evanston, Illinois, where his family had moved. There, with Northwestern University on one side and the sprawling city of Chicago on the other, he lived for the next seven years.

During that time, one of his closest friends was a scrawny little boy named Wally Cox. The scrawny boy grew into a scrawny man who became a very popular actor on his own. He is probably best remembered as the comical television star "Mr. Peepers."

The imp and the rebel were part of Marlon Brando even during these early years. The rebel showed itself in the way Marlon adjusted to school. He was intelligent, but he didn't like school, and he did badly because of it. The imp could be seen in his adventures with his friends. Once when they were playing "missionary and Indian,"

Marlon, the Indian, tied Wally Cox, the missionary, to a tree, then he went home. Several hours later a man found Cox still tied to the tree.

From Evanston, the family moved to Santa Ana, California. They stayed there for one year. Then they moved back to Libertyville, Illinois.

The Brandos bought a farm there. Marlon took care of the animals — geese, hens, rabbits, a horse, a cow, a Great Dane, and 28 cats. He said he wanted a raccoon for a pet. His parents said "No." He vowed one day to get a pet raccoon.

Marlon went to high school in Libertyville. His top interests at the time were playing on the school football team, acting with the school drama club, playing the drums, and riding horseback. Studies were nowhere on his list of likes, nor apparently was "good behavior." He spent many hours being kept after school as punishment.

Because he was doing very poorly, his father took him out of the public school. He sent Marlon to a military school in Minnesota.

Young, rebellious Marlon and the strict, Army-like school conducted their own little war from the very beginning. Marlon's weapons were practical jokes and his talent for mischief. The school's weapons were its punishment and its discipline. Marlon finally went down to defeat when the school ended the war during his junior year by expelling him.

His parents were very much upset, but there was not much they could do with the boy. Like so many others, then and later, they were unable truly to understand the young man.

Marlon Brando did not go back to school the next term. In fact, he never would receive a high school diploma.

Shortly after he had dropped out of school, the United States entered World War II. Marlon thought about joining the Army, but he was turned down because he had a bad knee and was very near-sighted.

Over the next few years, he worked as a laborer, a movie-theater usher, anything that was available. His parents wanted him to return to school and graduate, but they watched this hope fade.

In 1943 Marlon's mother took his two older sisters to New York City where they had both decided they wanted to live and seek careers. Shortly after, Marlon decided New York might be the place for him, too; so he joined his sisters; in fact, he moved in with them.

New York became his home until he would board that Santa Fe train for Hollywood six years later.

In New York, he decided to take some courses at the New School of Social Research. It was a college-level school, but a high school diploma was not required. The school was much different from the rigid, disciplined ones that he had attended before. In many ways, it was perfect for someone with the independent and rebellious nature of a Marlon Brando.

Among the courses he was taking were some in theater and acting. They were taught by Stella Adler, a wonderful teacher and an important person in the New York theater world.

Stella Adler taught acting in a way different from the usual. She taught "method acting." It was a very realistic form of acting. The actor had to *identify completely* with the character he was playing. Later Marlon Brando would live for weeks the life of a paraplegic, a man paralyzed from the waist down, because that was the part he had to play. In that way, he would develop his "method." Method acting really meant that the actor would "get inside" the character he was performing.

Once Marlon Brando came under the guidance of Stella Adler, he soon knew exactly what he wanted to do. He wanted to act.

He performed in a few shows at the school. Later, he played in a summer theater in upstate New York.

Only a little more than a year after he had arrived in New York, he won his first role in a Broadway play. It was in *I Remember Mama*. He played the part of one of Mama's sons, Nels. He was only 20 years old.

During those days, his old friend from Evanston, Wally Cox, moved to New York. Marlon had grown tired of living with his sisters. He and Cox agreed to get their own place.

Their apartment on Manhattan became a meeting place for all kinds of people at all times of day or night. There were unemployed actors and actresses, poets, musicians, folk singers, and just ordinary folks. Marlon played the bongos. He was the leader of such games as dropping water balloons from their window onto pedestrians walking below.

His second part in a Broadway show was in *Truckline Cafe*, by the famous playright, Maxwell Anderson. Marlon played a young man who murders his wife. The play lasted only two weeks. Marlon Brando, however, received praise for his acting.

The important thing about *Truckline Cafe* was that Marlon Brando made two new friends. One was another actor, Karl Malden.

The other was the director Elia Kazan. Marlon's friendship with Kazan would very shortly play an important part in his career.

After *Truckline Cafe,* Marlon acted in the George Bernard Shaw play *Candida.* After that, he was in Ben Hecht's *A Flag Is Born,* a flop. Then came *The Eagle Has Two Heads* with Tallulah Bankhead. They did not get along at all. After one performance, he was fired from the show.

Brando was becoming known around New York because of his acting, publicity agents and newspaper people began to interview him. He did not like the idea of people asking him about his personal life, so he told some he had been born in Calcutta, India. To others he mentioned he was born in Bangkok, Thailand. Still others learned from him that his birthplace was Rangoon, Burma.

During this time, Elia Kazan and Lee Strasburg began a school called Actors Studio. It was designed to teach and train new actors and actresses. The emphasis was on "method acting." Some of the students who would study there were Paul Newman, Joanne Woodward, Patricia Neal, Rod Steiger, James Dean, Shelley Winters, and Montgomery Clift. There were many other well-known names besides these, but their most famous student was also one of their first students — Marlon Brando.

Only a little more than a year after Marlon Brando first worked for Elia Kazan, he was offered the lead role in a new play Kazan was to direct. It was *A Streetcar Named Desire* by Tennessee Williams. The part was that of Stanley Kowalski, a rugged, crude, animal-like slob whose life becomes a mess when his sister-in-law comes to live with him and his wife. The part had been offered to John Garfield and later to other established actors, but they had all turned it down. Kazan suggested Brando. Brando tried out for the part. Everyone, including Tennessee Williams, thought he would work out.

Marlon Brando, 23 years old, had won the *lead* role in a Broadway play. With him in the show would be Jessica Tandy, an English actress, and two other friends from Actors Studio, Karl Malden and Kim Hunter.

Before Broadway, a play is "tried out" in another city first. There it is polished. Last minute changes are made. Then it is ready for New York. *A Streetcar Named Desire* was tried out in New Haven, Connecticut, in Boston, and in Philadelphia before it finally arrived on Broadway in 1947.

Opening night in New York is always a very special event. The success of a play is often determined by how the critics and the audience respond on opening night.

When the curtain closed on the opening night of *A Streetcar Named Desire,* the applause was tremendous. But what would the critics have to say? The cast, Tennessee Williams, Elia Kazan, and others involved with the show went to a nearby restaurant to wait for the early morning newspapers which would contain the reviews. When the papers were finally delivered, everyone nervously but quickly grabbed them up. For a few moments there was silence except for the rustling of newspapers. Then there were the sounds of joy and laughter. The reviews were excellent. Marlon Brando was hailed as a "great new young actor." The play went on to win the Pulitzer Prize for best drama of the year.

Marlon Brando was suddenly a major star at the age of 23.

One problem Marlon had, however, was the fact that he had a two-year contract for his role as Stanley Kowalski. Two years is an awfully long time to play the same role night after night. It was especially unhappy for someone like Marlon Brando, who was restless and always looking for new forms of excitement.

After about a year, he did earn a week's vacation. He was boxing, a new hobby, with one of the stagehands in the boiler room of the theater. He forgot to duck. The stagehand landed a neat left jab smack on the nose. Marlon's finely-shaped nose was now spread all over his face. It was broken.

The two years as Stanely Kowalski finally ended. Marlon Brando wanted to escape from the play, from New York, from everything in fact that had been part of the last two years. He was bored and restless so he went to Paris by himself. It was a city he had always wanted to see.

While in Europe, he received an offer from the well-known director, Stanley Kramer, to star in a movie. Called *The Men,* it was about the problems faced by paraplegic veterans returning from the war. Brando accepted the offer and a salary of $50,000.

Once in Hollywood, he moved in with some relatives. Shortly after, he went to the veterans' hospital where much of the movie was to be filmed. He moved in with the young veterans who, being paralyzed from the waist down, were confined to wheelchairs. Not only did he live with them, but he lived like them. In his own wheelchair he did everything that they did. It was his way of "getting inside" the part.

The veterans at first did not know quite what to think, but after a day or two, they realized that Marlon Brando was an exceptional young man. They found that he was as interested in them as human beings as they were in him as an actor. They grew to like him very much. He became fully accepted as part of their way of life. At times, some of them said, they completely forgot that he was *not* a paraplegic.

One evening they all went to a local tavern for a few beers. A woman approached them.

"You don't need those wheelchairs," she said. "No, you don't need them — not if you have faith in God. He'll cure you."

The men looked up. Everyone else in the place became silent.

"He can help you rise above your weakness," the woman continued. "All you need is faith in Him. Believe in Him and you can walk. You can do it."

Everyone seemed embarrassed. A man tried to get the woman to go back to her table. He pulled her toward it.

"Wait, I have faith," the paraplegic Marlon Brando said. "I . . . I can do it." The woman looked at him. His face was filled with great determination. "I can do it." He slowly lifted himself out of the wheelchair by the strength of his arms alone. "I can do it," he kept repeating in a faltering voice. He stood up. His legs were wobbling like a baby colt. The woman's eyes were as wide as saucers. Then he ran across the room and out of the tavern as fast as he could, shouting "I can do it. I can do it."

The Men, which opened in 1950, was a fine movie. Marlon Brando was praised for his role. He was a rising young movie star, everyone agreed.

16

After the filming was completed, Marlon went back to New York. He moved in again with Wally Cox. With him came a pet he had just acquired. He had finally got his pet raccoon.

The studio told Brando that he had to help publicize his film. He would have to talk to newspaper people and go on radio and television "talk" shows. It would help the movie to be successful. One interviewer came to ask a few questions. All Brando did was grunt in answer to each. The interviewer left shaking his head.

Brando told another that his best achievement was *not* the movie. Instead it was winning the Pulitzer Prize for fiction several years earlier. The reporter's newspaper printed the made-up story. On a television talk show in New York, he fell asleep — or at least pretended to — while the emcee was asking him questions.

Hollywood was not happy with its young rebel, but he was in demand. He was especially wanted for a movie that was being made at Warner Brothers and directed by Elia Kazan. It was the movie version of *A Streetcar Named Desire.* Brando was offered $75,000 to do the film. As his star was rising, so was his salary.

The cast for the movie was almost the same as the one for the Broadway play. Karl Malden and Kim Hunter were hired. The one person missing was the leading lady. Vivian Leigh replaced Jessica Tandy.

From the moment the movie opened in 1951, it was a tremendous success. The critics praised it. Brando's performance was called "great," "powerful," "filled with passion," and simply "excellent." To the studio's delight the movie was a great success at the box office as well.

In this, his second movie, Brando was nominated for the Academy Award for best actor. Other members of the cast were nominated for Oscars as well. On "Oscar night," Marlon's co-star, Vivian Leigh, won the award for best actress, and the Oscars for best supporting actor and actress went to Karl Malden and Kim Hunter for their roles in "Streetcar." Best actor, however, was awarded to Humphrey Bogart for his famous role of the grizzly boat captain in *The African Queen.*

By late 1951, Marlon Brando, only 27, was a major movie star. His face was known throughout the world. His "mumble" was just as well known. But beside being a star, he was also highly respected as a fine actor.

From "Streetcar" he went directly to another movie. It was a very different role. It was the part of Emiliano Zapata, a Mexican revolutionary hero. In a way, the part was perfect for Brando. Both he and Zapata were rebels, each in his own way. It was also an early illustration of the fact that Marlon Brando could and would play a dazzling variety of different characters during his movie career.

Viva Zapata was also being made by Elia Kazan. The script was being written by John Steinbeck, one of the greatest novelists in the United States who, a few short years later, would be awarded the highest honor in the world for literature, the Nobel Prize.

Marlon Brando again set out to "become the character." He went to live with the people of a small village in Mexico before filming began. Marlon worked hard at perfecting just the right Mexican accent. He personally supervised his own make-up. He wanted to "look" the part exactly, just as he wanted to "feel" it.

18

The movie, released in 1952, was another success, both critically and at the box office. Anthony Quinn who was in the movie with Brando won the Academy award as best supporting actor. Marlon Brando was again nominated as best actor, the second time in three years; but once again the Oscar escaped him. That year it was awarded to Gary Cooper for his role as the lonely and brave sheriff in *High Noon.*

Stardom had not helped Marlon Brando to settle down. His behavior was as strange as ever. During the filming of "Zapata," an interviewer asking Brando a question was as likely to get a belch as an answer. He had also taken up yoga. Now he was often seen sitting in a yoga "squat" or standing on his head — in front of the hotel where he was staying, on the movie set, in front of interviewers, almost anywhere in fact. He had also revived his sport of throwing water balloons at people.

Again Marlon returned to New York where he still kept an apartment. He did not like living in Hollywood, Beverly Hills, or anywhere else out in Southern California where the other movie stars lived. On the other hand, he did not like New York either, but he felt more at home there.

Then he was tempted with a new and considerably different type of movie role. He was offered the part of Marc Antony in the movie version of the classic Shakespearian play *Julius Caesar.* He accepted.

In the movie, he would be acting with some of the finest names in the classical theater — John Gielgud, Louis Calhern, James Mason. Many critics, however, wondered aloud whether the "mumbling, method actor" would be completely out of place in a Shakespearian play. Some even said that Brando had been cast in the role only because, as a star, he would bring out to see the movie people who ordinarily would not have come.

Marlon Brando did not feel that way, however. Once again he thrust himself into the role he would play. He obviously could not go back to ancient Rome or to Shakespeare's England, but he did the next best thing. He studied hour after hour for weeks under a classical drama coach. At the same time he listened to every available record of persons who had played Mark Antony. Brando was most influenced by the British actor Laurence Olivier. It is said that Brando listened to Olivier's performance hundreds of times before he tried the part himself.

Marlon Brando on the set of *Julius Caesar* was not the same Marlon Brando who fooled around on the sets of his three previous movies. He was very serious about his role. Gone were the pranks, the jokes, the clowning.

The movie opened in New York in 1953. There, on screen, was Marlon Brando dressed in a white toga. His Roman sandals criss-crossed their way up his legs to the knees. His hair was in curly bangs. He looked as though he really could have been Mark Antony. The critics were amazed. There was no typical Marlon Brando mumble. No words were slurred as they were in his other "method" roles. But at the same time he was a unique and highly interesting Mark Antony. He gave the famous speech of Antony after the death of Caesar: "Friends, Romans, countrymen. Lend me your ears . . .," and the movie world did. He was praised by his fellow actors and by the critics.

For the third time in four years, Marlon Brando was nominated for the Academy Award for best actor. That alone was a remarkable achievement for an actor who was not yet 30 years old.

1953 was the year of a fine war movie, *From Here to Eternity*. The movie and the people associated with it won every major award, except one — best actor. Again, however, that was not to go to Marlon Brando. It was awarded to William Holden for his part in *Stalag 17*.

Some people were beginning to say that Brando would never get the award. The reason was simple. He was a rebel. He did not go along with the "Hollywood way of doing things." He even spoke out against Hollywood. Therefore he had been punished over the past years, and he would continue to be punished; that is, unless he changed his ways. Brando ignored the entire situation. When asked about it, he would simply shrug his shoulders.

In his next movie, which was actually made before *Julius Caesar* was released, he played the role of a motorcycle gang leader in *The Wild One*. He traded his toga and sandals for a black leather jacket and motorcycle boots. This movie, however, was not a success. It contained a large amount of violence. Just the thought of motor- cycle gangs made people fearful. Besides, it just wasn't as good as the movies Marlon Brando had starred in before. At the same time, it did have some good points. It was the first of its kind — a movie that showed *real* threats to the society of the time. It paved the way for such very good movies as *Blackboard Jungle* and *Rebel Without a Cause* which would come out in the next few years.

Elia Kazan then came back on the scene. He told Marlon he had a role that was perfect for him — a role in a film to be called *On the Waterfront*. Marlon listened to the story. It was about the horrors of working on the docks in New York. The unions, controlled by the crime syndicate, treat the individual workers miserably. The movie was a protest against this. It had a "message." Brando loved the idea.

The script would be written by one of America's best writers, Budd Schulberg. The background music would be composed by Leonard Bernstein. Acting with Brando would be his friend, Karl Malden, and three other fine actors from the Actors Studio — Rod Steiger, Lee J. Cobb, and Eva Marie Saint. Elia Kazan would direct.

Brando would play the leading role — Terry Malloy, a one-time, small-time boxer who now works on the docks. Malloy is in love with a girl (Eva Marie Saint), but he betrays her brother to the union, thinking that the brother would just get beaten up. The brother, however, is killed. Malloy feels guilty. He begins to talk about the murder and who might have done it. The union and the crime syndicate learn that Malloy has been talking about it. They send Malloy's brother (Rod Steiger), who works for the union, to tell him to shut up . . . or else.

The brother does not get the chance. Instead, Malloy tells him how badly he feels about what has happened. Not only that, he tells about how the crime syndicate had gotten him to throw a fight when he was boxing. In doing it, he had destroyed his boxing career. The words of Terry Malloy, spoken with deep emotion, are among the most famous that Marlon Brando ever muttered on the screen. The pain of what Malloy did and what he lost by it are stamped into the face of Brando as he explains, "Oh, Charley . . . Charley. You don't understand. I coulda had class. I coulda been a contender. I coulda been somebody . . . instead of a bum, which is what I am."

Charley is killed because he failed to stop Malloy from talking. Terry Malloy goes on to testify in court about the corruption and crime on the docks. Then he goes back to the docks. The dock workers are afraid to stand with him. He faces and fights the union boss (Lee J. Cobb). It is one of the most brutal fights in movie history. Malloy survives. He has faced down the union and its criminal friends. The dock workers rally behind him.

On the Waterfront was a very good movie. In fact, it will go down in movie history as a great movie. The critics raved about it. People flocked to see it. It was the smash hit of 1954.

Marlon Brando received his fourth nomination for an Academy Award for best actor. Many of the highest praises about the movie had been for his acting. He was the definite favorite to win the award, but would Hollywood give it to him, or would Hollywood "punish" him once again for being the rebel?

If he did win the award, what would he do? What would he say? Would he appear on stage in levis and a T-shirt? Would he stand on his head before the audience? Would he say nasty things about Hollywood and the movie industry? He was capable of any and all of these things, most people in Hollywood agreed. They had no idea what to expect from the rebel in their midst.

The night the Oscars were awarded, the audience became absolutely silent before the announcement, "The award for best

actor goes to. . . . Marlon Brando for his role in *On The Waterfront*." Hollywood had decided not to deny him any longer its highest award.

Marlon Brando trotted down the aisle and up onto the stage. Believe it or not, the rebel was dressed in a tuxedo. He took the Oscar, looked at it and then paused.

There was the trace of a smile on his face as he looked back at the audience. "Uh . . . uh . . ." the sound was that of the now-famous Brando mumble. "It's much heavier than I imagined . . ." A few more words, and then he said simply and warmly, "It's a wonderful moment . . . and a rare one . . . and I'm certainly indebted. Thank you."

The rebel was nowhere in sight that evening.

On The Waterfront also brought Academy Awards to Eva Marie Saint for best supporting actress, to Elia Kazan for best director, to Budd Schulberg for best screen play. The movie itself won the award for the best picture of the year.

After the awards, Marlon Brando's career was at its highest point. He was an established superstar.

But the fame and the wealth that came with being a superstar were not easy for him to handle. He still intensely disliked publicity. He wanted no one to intrude on his private life. He did not want them to know him as a person, but it was next to impossible to avoid the spotlight when you were a superstar.

Around the same time, his mother died. She was the first person in his immediate family to die, and Marlon was deeply saddened.

Despite his success, everything seemed to be crowding in on him.

He was not at all happy, so he returned once again to New York, but this time, he stayed very much to himself. He did not answer letters or even offers for new movies. He did not answer the telephone. He was interested in "causes," in helping people; but he wasn't sure how to do it. What he did know was that, for him at least, life had to have more meaning than just acting or just being a superstar.

After "Waterfront," Marlon accepted the role of Napoleon in *Desiree.* The movie was a flop both to the critics and at the box office. It was the first real failure that Brando had been associated with since he began in the movies five years earlier.

The next year, 1955, Marlon Brando accepted the *most* different role of his career. He would star in the musical comedy *Guys and Dolls* with Frank Sinatra, Jean Simmons, and Vivian Blaine. Brando had never before sung and danced in a musical. As Sky Masterson, a slangy New York gambler dressed in a black suit, black shirt, and white tie, Marlon Brando made his musical debut.

While making the movie, the two superstars — Brando and Sinatra — got along like two sharks going after the same meal. By the time the movie was completed, they barely spoke to each other.

The movie was a success financially but not critically. Brando decided never again to make a musical.

The year 1956 brought Brando another highly different role. He agreed to play the oriental houseboy in a comedy called *Teahouse of the August Moon.* The show had been a very successful Broadway play.

There were a number of problems. First Brando had to lose 20 pounds. Then came make-up. It took almost two hours every morning to make up his face so that he would look like an oriental. He also had to master a proper Asian accent.

During the filming of this movie, Brando got along no better with his co-star, Glenn Ford, than he had with Frank Sinatra.

Word was getting around that Marlon Brando was becoming even more difficult to work with. Even worse, his antics were costing the film studios a good deal of money by delaying production of the movie.

When Academy Award time came around, Marlon's name was not mentioned. In his last three movies now, he had failed to receive an Oscar nomination.

The next movie, however, got Marlon Brando back on the track to the Oscar. It was *Sayonara*. The movie had a message, one which Brando liked. It was about the difficulties American servicemen encountered in trying to bring their Japanese wives back to America in the years after World War II. Brando played an American Air Force officer who falls in love with a young Japanese girl. The movie was successful. Brando won his fifth nomination for an Academy Award as best actor. The award was given, however, to the English actor Alec Guinness for his role as the persecuted prisoner in *The Bridge On the River Kwai*.

About this time, Marlon Brando established his own production company. His father, a good businessman, was put in charge of it. It was called Pennebaker Productions. Marlon was now earning a tremendous amount of money. He had earned more than a million dollars from his movies.

He had also met a mysterious young lady from India during those

days. Her name was Anna Kashfi. They were often seen together. Brando was still a bachelor at 33.

The same year, 1957, he took on another movie, *The Young Lions*. He dyed his hair blond for the role of a young German Nazi officer in World War II. In his eight-year career in Hollywood, he had now played a German officer, the French Napoleon, a Mexican revolutionary, an ancient Roman, and an Asian houseboy. He was becoming, it seemed, a one-man United Nations.

The Young Lions was a good movie. It was, however, the last successful movie Brando would make for many years.

In October, 1957, he surprised everyone by announcing that he and Anna Kashfi had gotten married. She claimed to be a native of India, and she dressed in the typical Indian *sari*. Not everyone believed her, however; especially when a couple, living in the British Isles, said she was their daughter, and they were "as English as the London Bridge," they said. They produced a birth certificate which, they claimed, was hers. Anna, the mysterious one, denied it.

Before 1957 was over, however, the newly-married couple separated. A son was born in 1958. The Brandos never again lived together. They were formally divorced in 1958. Apparently married life was not the life for Marlon Brando.

While all this was going on, Brando began work on a movie for his own production company. It would be a Western, and he would star in it. Script writers were put to work. Stanley Kubrick was hired to direct the movie. He was a young director who had made several good movies. Later he would make such famous movies as *Dr. Strangelove* and *2001: A Space Odyssey*.

The group met almost daily in Marlon's new home in California to work on the movie. It was a Japanese-style house. In keeping with his new house, Marlon required everyone to take off their shoes before they could enter. Then they would all sit on pillows on the floor. Marlon, often dressed in a Japanese robe, would call the group to order by striking a large Japanese gong.

Marlon himself became involved very much in the writing of the movie. As time went on, he found he was arguing constantly with his director. They just could not agree. Finally Marlon fired Kubrick and announced that he would direct the movie himself.

During the same period of time, Marlon signed on to do another movie based on a play by Tennessee Williams. Brando and Williams had not worked together since *A Streetcar Named Desire.* The new movie was *The Fugitive Kind.* In it, Brando played another slob — a brooding Southerner, dressed in a real snakeskin jacket, who wanders about playing the guitar. The movie opened in 1960. It was a failure. It lost money, and it got terrible reviews.

Work continued on Brando's own movie, *One-Eyed Jacks,* but it was going slowly. It was also beginning to cost a lot more money than everyone thought it would. As a director, Marlon Brando was slowing down production by filming scenes over and over again until they were just exactly the way he wanted them. When he was finally through, he had spent more than $6 million. The original budget for the movie was less than $2 million. The result was a movie that was almost five hours long. It had to be cut. Brando tried and tried. But he could not get it down to a reasonable two hours. Finally he just left it for someone else to cut. He was through with his own movie.

The movie was finally released in 1961. It had taken four years from the time the first script had been written. The movie had many fine scenes, but it was not a success.

Marlon Brando then signed up to star in the biggest production of his life. He would play Mr. Christian, the leading role in a new version of *Mutiny on the Bounty.* It was to be a huge spectacular. No expense was to be spared. The movie budget was $10 million.

Filming began in late 1960. Again there were delays. Most were blamed on Marlon Brando. He was impossible to work with, many said. The months wore on. The costs kept rolling in. Finally, in late 1963, three years later, the movie was ready. However, it had cost $25 million to make instead of the $10 million budgeted. The studio, Metro-Goldwyn-Mayer (MGM), almost went into bankruptcy because of it.

Hollywood's rebel had now become an intolerable problem. He may have been a superstar, but the studios could no longer afford him. Word was getting out; the troubles and costs that came with him were just not worth it.

The offers did not stop, however. They just were not for "big-time" movies, like they had been before.

The change in his fortune did not really bother Marlon Brando. He now was devoting a lot of time to causes other than acting. He became very active in the civil rights movement. He went all over the country working for the cause. He participated in marches and demonstrations, and he gave speeches. He even talked to the press and radio and television people — about civil rights, however, not about acting or himself personally.

He spoke out against the role the United States was playing in Southeast Asia. He was strongly against our involvement in the war there. But the cause he was most involved with was the one regarding the American Indian. He felt they were the most mistreated of all Americans. He devoted his strongest efforts to improve their situation.

Marlon Brando was now the owner of a small group of islands near Tahiti in the South Pacific. It was here he could find peace and quiet and the privacy he so often wanted. It was here he would go to escape.

During the 9-year period, 1963 to 1971, Marlon Brando made 11 movies. None were big successes. One or two might be considered good movies (*Reflections in a Golden Eye* and *The Ugly American*). Most of the movies were bad and were quickly forgotten. Just look at the list:

The Ugly American	*1963*
Bedtime Story	1964
The Saboteur: MoriTuri	1965
The Chase	1966
The Appaloosa	1966
A Countess from Hong Kong	1967
Reflections in a Golden Eye	1967
Candy	1968
The Night of the Following Day	1969
Burn	1970
The Nightcomers	1971

The movies themselves may not have been good, yet Marlon

Brando's acting was still good. He might be a problem. He might irritate many people. He might be a rebel with many causes. But he was still a fine actor. No one could deny him that. In 1972, he proved that once again in a spectacular way.

A young director named Francis Ford Coppola wanted Marlon Brando for the lead role in a movie he was making. It was *The Godfather,* the story of the powerful head of a crime syndicate organization.

Brando decided he would like the part. But in 1972 times were different. The studios no longer wanted the rebel. He would automatically bring trouble, they said. On top of it, he had not made a truly successful movie in the last 10 years. They could not forget *Mutiny on the Bounty* and *One-Eyed Jacks,* and the tremendous costs of the two movies.

Paramount Studio said it did not want Brando. Anybody else, they said, but not Marlon Brando. Coppola argued. Finally the studios agreed, but only if two conditions were met. Brando would have to

take a screen test for the part, and he would only be paid a percentage of the profits, not a salary as well.

It was unheard of to ask an established superstar to take a screen test for a role, but they did ask, and Brando took it. He also agreed to work without a salary.

Marlon Brando threw himself into the role completely. It was like the old days of "Streetcar," "Waterfront," and "Caesar." He spent hours working on his make-up. He used rubber cement to make his face look old. Tissue paper and cotton were stuffed into his cheeks to fatten his face. He "became" the strong and powerful old man who was iron-fisted in the world of crime, but whose hand was soft and gentle with his own family.

When the movie opened, Brando's performance as the "Godfather" was praised by the critics. It was the most powerful single thing in a tremendously good movie. The movie was a sudden success. It would earn in one year more money than any other movie in the history of motion pictures.

Before *The Godfather* had even been released, however, Brando went to Paris to star in another movie. The name of it was *Last Tango in Paris.* It was very different from *The Godfather;* but it, too, would be successful. It, too, would earn millions of dollars for its producers and for its star Marlon Brando.

After filming it, however, Brando quickly went back to his island in Tahiti.

He learned that for his role in *The Godfather,* he had been nominated for the Academy Award for best actor. It was the sixth time he had been nominated for the high award, but it had been a long time since he was nominated — 15 years, in fact.

No one could find out how he felt about the nomination, however. He was on his island, and he would not talk to anyone from the outside.

Academy Award night came to Hollywood. Marlon Brando did not. Brando won the Oscar for best actor. Hollywood's most famous rebel, however, refused to accept the award.

A young American Indian girl, Sasheen Littlefeather, went on stage when it was announced that he had won. She said that Marlon Brando would not accept the award in protest of the way the Indian had been shown in movies and television over the years.

She was not able to finish reading a statement explaining his views. The audience of actors and actresses, directors, producers, and other celebrities booed. She finally had to leave the stage.

Other people in the motion picture business were not at all happy with Marlon Brando, but then they never really had been. They could not understand why he behaved the way he did, but then they never had been able to understand him or his behavior.

What they had to admit, however, was that he was a talented actor whose performances commanded respect. He was unique. Like the writer Ernest Hemingway, he had his own style. Many would try to copy him. Many — like James Dean, Paul Newman, Steve McQueen, and Jack Nicholson, to name only a few — were strongly influenced by his style of acting, but also like Hemingway, no one could do it quite like the master, the originator himself. Nor does it seem likely anyone in the future will ever truly understand the great actor and notorious rebel named Marlon Brando.